GrowinG
P A I N S

BIBLE STUDY GUIDE

From the Bible-teaching ministry of

Charles R. Swindoll

INSIGHT FOR LIVING

Charles R. Swindoll is a graduate of Dallas Theological Seminary and has served in pastorates in Texas, Massachusetts, and California since 1963. He has served as senior pastor of the First Evangelical Free Church of Fullerton, California, since 1971. Chuck's radio program, "Insight for Living," began in 1979. In addition to his church and radio ministries, Chuck enjoys writing. He has authored numerous books and booklets on a variety of subjects.

Based on the outlines and transcripts of Chuck's sermons, the study guide text is coauthored by Lee Hough, a graduate of the University of Texas at Arlington and Dallas Theological Seminary. The Living Insights are written by Bill Butterworth, a graduate of Florida Bible College, Dallas Theological Seminary, and Florida Atlantic University.

Editor in Chief: Cynthia Swindoll	**Director, Communications Division:** Carla Beck
Coauthor of Text: Lee Hough	**Project Manager:** Alene Cooper
Author of Living Insights: Bill Butterworth	**Art Director:** Steve Mitchell
Assistant Editor: Glenda Schlahta	**Designer:** Gary Lett
Copy Manager: Jac La Tour	**Production Artists:** Gary Lett and Diana Vasquez
Copyediting Supervisor: Marty Anderson	**Typographer:** Bob Haskins
Copy Editor: Marty Anderson	**Print Production Manager:** Deedee Snyder

ISBN 0-8499-8409-2

Printed in the United States of America.

COVER PHOTOGRAPH: Rudi Weislein

CONTENTS

INTRODUCTION

I have a T-shirt an athletic coach gave me a couple of years ago. In bold letters these words appear on the back:

NO GAIN WITHOUT PAIN

So true! Growing up also includes times of pain. Nobody ever escapes the process. We simply *cannot* become the people God meant us to be without some headaches and heartaches. Even Jesus our Lord "learned obedience from the things which He suffered" (Hebrews 5:8).

This is a realistic series of biblical messages about life in God's family . . . a life of disappointments, mistakes, struggles, hardships, and misunderstandings. Not a moment, however, is spent apart from God's watchful eye. Hopefully, each message will bring you reassurance and renewed determination to hang tough.

The road from earth to heaven is not an easy, downhill slide. It is, rather, a challenge that forces us to look to Him who has gone before us. He *will* see us through! Each tough experience simply reminds us we are on the right road.

Chuck Swindoll

Chuck Swindoll

PUTTING TRUTH INTO ACTION

K nowledge apart from application falls short of God's desire for His children. He wants us to apply what we learn so that we will change and grow. This study guide was prepared with these goals in mind. As you go through the following pages, we hope your desire to discover biblical truth will grow as your understanding of God's Word increases, and that you will be encouraged to apply what you've learned.

To assist you in your study, we've included a section called Living Insights at the end of each lesson. These exercises will challenge you to study further and to think of specific ways to put your discoveries into action.

There are many ways to use this guide—in personal devotions, group studies, discussions with friends and family, and Sunday school classes. And, of course, it's an ideal study aid when you're listening to its corresponding "Insight for Living" radio series.

To benefit most from this study guide, we would encourage you to consider it a spiritual journal. That's why we've included space in the Living Insights for recording your thoughts and discoveries. We hope you'll return to those sections often for review and encouragement as you continue to grow in your walk with Christ.

Lee Hough
Coauthor of Text

Bill Butterworth
Author of Living Insights

GrowinG
PAINS

Chapter 1

GROWING THROUGH WAITING

Psalm 62:1–2, 5–8

Richard Foster, in *Celebration of Discipline*, says, "Superficiality is the curse of our age. The doctrine of instant satisfaction is a primary spiritual problem. The desperate need today is not for a greater number of intelligent people, or gifted people, but for deep people."[1]

The psalmist describes this kind of deep person as being like "a tree firmly planted by streams of water, Which yields its fruit in its season, And its leaf does not wither" (Ps. 1:3).

As Foster pointed out, the number of firmly rooted trees on the Christian landscape is growing smaller, and it's largely because of an unwillingness to wait on God. We tend to replace waiting on God with hurried attempts at pursuing growth on our own. And so we settle for shallow roots destined to yield only mediocre growth. Carl G. Jung once said, "Hurry is not *of* the Devil; it *is* the Devil."[2] And the more we graft this attitude of hurry into our pursuit of God, the more it stunts the growth of our inner being. Our physical stature may mature over the years, but there will be only a few rings of maturity in our godly character.

Biblical Examples of "Waiters"

To begin our journey into the subject of waiting on God, let's take a brisk walk through some of the redwoods of the faith—

---

1. Richard J. Foster, *Celebration of Discipline* (San Francisco, Calif.: Harper and Row, Publishers, 1978), p. 1.

2. As quoted by Foster in *Celebration of Discipline*, p. 13.

ordinary people who became spiritual giants because they chose to wait on God.

Noah

God told Noah to build the ark because He planned to send a rain to cleanse the earth for a new beginning. Enduring his neighbor's derision and perhaps his own doubts, Noah waited 120 years before that rain—the earth's first—finally came.

Job

Job's gnarly trunk is deeply scarred where he lost his family, his wealth, and his own health in one of the most well-known examples of undeserved suffering recorded in the Bible. One by one the physical, emotional, financial, and spiritual supports for his faith were removed, prompting his wife to suggest he curse God and die. But throughout this time when Job's pain seemed endless, he chose instead to wait on the Lord.

Abraham

At the age of seventy-five a very prosperous and settled Abraham left his native land, guided only by God's promise, "I will make you a great nation" (Gen. 11:27–12:4). And for more than one hundred years Abraham waited on God, continually pulling up his tent pegs and moving, always looking toward the day God would tell him to throw away the canvas and pour a cement foundation.

Joseph

Joseph endured fourteen years inside a dark Egyptian prison cell for a crime he didn't commit. But rather than withering and dying, he solidified the green timber of his faith by waiting on God and trusting in His sovereignty.

Moses

Moses, the adopted son of Pharaoh's daughter, was well educated, a prestigious bright star of Egypt. But at the age of forty, he killed an Egyptian and was forced to flee for his life. For the next forty years this military leader and powerful speaker lived alone in a desert learning to wait on God. It was a time of replacing Moses' trust in himself to get things done with trusting and waiting on God.

Paul

Paul had grown to be one of the tallest trees the religious system of the Pharisees could produce. And when Christians began sprouting up in his neck of the woods, he zealously led the persecution to cut them down. But Christ had other plans for Paul. In a humbling encounter, the axe was laid to the roots of his Pharisaism, and Paul was grafted by faith into Christianity. Finding himself a seedling again, Paul spent the next three years alone, growing in his knowledge and understanding of his new Savior, whom he would wait on for the rest of his life.

Jesus

Just before Christ's public ministry began, Satan offered Him all the kingdoms of the world if He would only worship him. In this last of three tests, Satan tempted Christ to receive glory and power in a way other than God's way, which was to be through the Cross (Phil. 2:8–11, Matt. 28:18). Christ, however, was willing to wait, to endure suffering, and to become the sacrifice for our sin, in order to receive back His seat at the right hand of the Father.

Initial Observations about Waiting

Let's catch our breath for just a moment and make two observations about our topic.

Waiting on God is the rule instead of the exception.

All of us have a natural tendency to make waiting on God the exception and trusting in our own wisdom the rule; when there are no open doors, we try to force the locks. But open doors—like the ones that finally ended Job's pain, released Joseph from prison, and made it possible for Moses to lead the Israelites out of Egypt—don't always come along the minute we want them. We must learn to accept the fact that, in many areas of our lives, waiting will be the very process God uses to mature us.

Waiting on God is resting, not worrying.

The difference between waiting and worrying is focus. When we are truly waiting on the Lord, our posture and attitude are like Mary's as she sat at the Lord's feet, giving Him her undivided attention. When we worry, we're more like Martha who, although busy serving the Lord, was distracted and anxious. The point is that no matter whether we're feeling alienated because of our impulsive mistakes or trapped by unjust accusations or surrounded by intense suffering, we can all join Mary at the Savior's feet at any time.

> Be anxious for nothing, but in everything by prayer and supplication with thanksgiving let your requests be made known to God. And the peace of God, which surpasses all comprehension, shall guard your hearts and your minds in Christ Jesus. (Phil. 4:6–7)

3

Personal Exhortation to Wait

Reaching into the intimate psalmody of his heart during a crisis, David transposed his faith into a song that gives encouragement to other "waiters."

> My soul waits in silence for God only;
> From Him is my salvation.
> He only is my rock and my salvation,
> My stronghold; I shall not be greatly shaken. . . .
> My soul, wait in silence for God only,
> For my hope is from Him.
> He only is my rock and my salvation,
> My stronghold; I shall not be shaken.
> On God my salvation and my glory rest;
> The rock of my strength, my refuge is in God.
> Trust in Him at all times, O people;
> Pour out your heart before Him;
> God is a refuge for us. (Ps. 62:1–2, 5–8)

What to Do

David beckons us to do two things.

Wait for God to direct your steps (vv. 1a, 5a). First, David declares this statment, and later he reminds himself of it—just the way we need reminding when we feel our hearts beginning to grow restless.

Trust God to provide for your needs (vv. 1–2). Someone has said that our greatest strengths can also be our greatest weaknesses, and this is especially true when it comes to trusting God to provide for us. We're only too happy to lift up needs in the areas of our weaknesses. But when it comes to the areas of our strengths, our needs are reluctantly lifted up, and then only after we have exhausted all our skills in trying to provide for ourselves.

How to Wait

David also imparts two ways to practice waiting.

In silence (vv. 1, 5). Some of the best times we may ever spend in prayer are the ones when we stop talking and simply listen. Times when we meditate upon the things of the Lord. During these times God may bring to mind a needed truth, a praise, something to be thankful for, or a practical application of His Word that we had been missing.

In stability and confidence (vv. 2, 6). The prophet Isaiah put it this way:

Yet those who wait for the Lord
Will gain new strength;
They will mount up with wings like eagles,
They will run and not get tired,
They will walk and not become weary. (Isa. 40:31)

The Hebrew word for *wait* here is *qavah*, which means "to twist, to stretch, to become strong." It's the idea of twisting one thing around another so that greater strength will result, like a rope. By waiting on God, we are entwining ourselves around His character, joining ourselves to a stability and confidence we do not possess on our own.

Why Wait?

David's psalm is ripe with the fruits that come from waiting on God. They include *deliverance*, "From Him is my salvation" (Ps. 62:1); *security*, "He only is my rock . . . my stronghold" (v. 2); *hope*, "My hope is from Him" (v. 5); *glory*, "On God my salvation and my glory rest" (v. 7); and *refuge*, "My refuge is in God" (v. 7).

Practical Application for Today

A student once asked the president of his school if there was a course he could take that was shorter than the one prescribed. "Oh yes," replied the president, "but then it depends upon what you want to be. When God wants to make an oak, He takes a hundred years, but when He wants to make a squash, He takes six months."[3]

Many of us, while waiting on God, have asked a similar question, "Lord, isn't there a shorter, less difficult route I could take?"

But it's only by waiting on Him—trusting, praying, resting—that our roots will go deep enough for us to be as solid as an oak, to have the patience of a sequoia, to acquire the wisdom of a two-hundred-foot pine, and to possess the quiet humility of an aspen.

Living Insights   STUDY ONE

Psalm 62 is a song with a clear theme—waiting on God. Even a casual glance at the words shows the advantage of trusting God over your own strength.

- Let's take a closer look at Psalm 62. In the space provided, put the meaning of the listed terms in your own words. Then consult

3. Miles J. Stanford, *Principles of Spiritual Growth* (Lincoln, Neb.: Back to the Bible, 1977), p. 12.

a Bible dictionary or a cross-reference in Scripture to broaden your understanding of the meaning of this passage.

Psalm 62

Rock, verse 2

Your description: _____

_____

Reference definition: _____

_____

Stronghold, verse 2

Your description: _____

_____

Reference definition: _____

_____

Hope, verse 5

Your description: _____

_____

Reference definition: _____

_____

Refuge, verse 7

Your description: _____

_____

Reference definition: _____

_____

Trust, verse 8

Your description: _____

_____

Reference definition: _____

_____

It's one thing to read a psalm about waiting, and quite another to be involved in the waiting process. We'll use the next few minutes to personalize the truths we've been studying.

- Are you waiting right now? Are you trying to pull something off in your own strength? Describe your present situation.

_____

_____

_____

_____

- There are three direct applications to be found in verse 8 of Psalm 62. How are they acted out in your life?

  1. Waiting involves *trusting.*
     How can I exercise greater trust this week?

     _____

     _____

     _____

  2. Waiting includes *praying.*
     How seriously have I poured out my heart to God?

     _____

     _____

     _____

  3. Waiting implies *resting.*
     Am I anxious, tense, worrisome? In what areas can I practice resting this week?

     _____

     _____

     _____

- Spend a little time now in prayer. If necessary, confess to God your shortcomings in approaching your situation. Ask for His help in being still. Ask Him for the wisdom to wait.

Chapter 2

GROWING THROUGH FAILURE

Psalm 103

Sometime ago the *Fort Worth Star-Telegram* ran an article about an interesting notice that was spotted in a small-town barbecue restaurant.

> REWARD: Lost dog. Three legs, blind in left eye, right ear missing, tail broken, recently neutered. Answers to the name "Lucky."

If it's true that we can grow from our mistakes and failures, ol' Lucky must have been either a mighty smart dog or a real slow learner!

What makes the difference between being smart or a slow learner? What makes it possible for personal growth to rise up out of the deadness of a failed marriage, bankrupt business, or floundering walk with the Lord?

Our response. Surely, if Satan can get Christians preoccupied with their failures, then the opportunity for growth can be delayed indefinitely.

So how does one grow from an experience of failure? That's what we'll be studying today.

Initial Facts about Failure

Part of the reason failure is so painful is that it is usually accompanied by two pressures that really work us over.

Pressure from Other People

It's painful being kicked when you're down, but in many churches this back-alley treatment seems to be a sanctioned indoor sport. At a time when restoration is needed, many continue to be pummeled with blame. The pointed fingers of padded-pew quarterbacks seem to outnumber the helping hands of fellow bruised players on the field.

Pressure from Self

Many of us have tried to pattern ourselves after the image of the super-Christian which the church has unfortunately fostered. So when we fall short of this false ideal, we heap guilt on ourselves for being anything less than perfect. Our consciences, being more attuned to this fallacy than to a forgiving God, stand ready to fire when any semblance of humanity exposes itself.

Practical Ways to Recover from Failure

Jesus said, "Come to Me, all who are weary and heavy-laden, and I will give you rest" (Matt. 11:28). And when you're carrying around a load of failure on your shoulders, that's just the invitation you need.

In Psalm 103, David gave us the encouraging and practical counsel we need to come to Christ and put down that load. His advice centers around five crucial areas.

Responsibility: *Your reaction is your responsibility.*

David's psalm bursts open with an admonition to himself and to us that ensures a healthy reaction to failure.

> Bless the Lord, O my soul;
> And all that is within me, bless His holy name.
> Bless the Lord, O my soul,
> And forget none of His benefits. (vv. 1–2)

The first thing we have to come to grips with is our reaction to failure. The natural human tendency is to search for a source of blame, but David repeatedly emphasizes the importance of fixing our eyes on the Lord. Where we place our eyes during times of failure will make the difference between bitterness, moodiness, and anger, or humility and growth.

Focus: *Replace blaming yourself with claiming God's grace.*

While we often blame others for our failures, our next favorite hobby seems to be beating up on ourselves. David offers an encouraging alternative—remember the Lord,

> Who pardons all your iniquities;
> Who heals all your diseases;
> Who redeems your life from the pit;
> Who crowns you with lovingkindness and compassion;
> Who satisfies your years with good things,
> So that your youth is renewed like the eagle. . . .
> He has not dealt with us according to our sins,
> Nor rewarded us according to our iniquities.
> For as high as the heavens are above the earth,

So great is His lovingkindness toward those who fear
   Him.
As far as the east is from the west,
So far has He removed our transgressions from us.
(vv. 3–5, 10–12)

Second Corinthians 5:17 says, "Therefore if any man is in Christ, he is a new creature; the old things passed away; behold, new things have come." In these verses from Psalm 103, David pours out the new things that God's love and grace provide. So often the only thing blocking us from the love of God is ourselves. We think God's love is given only when certain conditions are met. If we don't make mistakes, if we read our Bibles every day, if we pray regularly, we think God will be happy with us and love us. But if we fail to do such things, we feel that He will withhold His love. This is a lie from the devil that keeps us from acknowledging and receiving the gifts of God's grace that He holds out to us all.

Security: Count on the Lord's constant understanding and complete forgiveness.

When the things we count on for security fail—such as a job, a relationship, a life's dream—our whole world seems to crumble with them. David points us to the only kind of security that will never let us down.

Just as a father has compassion on his children,
So the Lord has compassion on those who fear Him.
For He Himself knows our frame;
He is mindful that we are but dust. (vv. 13–14)

Much of our discouragement in failure comes from focusing on people. We tend to base our security on whether or not others will accept us, and that acceptance, we feel, is usually based on our performance. When we succeed, we believe we are loved and wanted; but when we fail, we have to get back up to a certain level of performance before we feel accepted again.

Unfortunately, this is the type of insecurity many of us live with. But with God, there is always constant understanding and complete forgiveness. He already knows our hearts, our motives, our worst failings, and yet He continues to love us.

Perspective: Refuse to compare yourself with any other person.

When failure hits, one of the first casualties is our perspective. In verses 15–18, David contrasts man with God and offers insight into how we can hold on to the right perspective.

As for man, his days are like grass;
As a flower of the field, so he flourishes.
When the wind has passed over it, it is no more;
And its place acknowledges it no longer.
But the lovingkindness of the Lord is from everlasting
to everlasting on those who fear Him,
And His righteousness to children's children,
To those who keep His covenant,
And who remember His precepts to do them.

One of the things we are tempted to do when we fail is to compare ourselves with others, which only increases our despair and self-pity. We look at the neighbor who's never lost his job; we look at newer Christians who seem further along in their maturity. And the longer we look, the more distorted our perspective becomes concerning our problems. But David reminds us that people come and go like short-lived flowers and that the Lord's loving-kindness is everlasting. It's His judgment and His perspective that count.

Morale: *Continue to obey the Lord.*

David began by telling himself to focus on the Lord. Now he concludes by broadening his admonition to include even the angels.

The Lord has established His throne in the heavens;
And His sovereignty rules over all.
Bless the Lord, you His angels,
Mighty in strength, who perform His word,
Obeying the voice of His word!
Bless the Lord, all you His hosts,
You who serve Him, doing His will.
Bless the Lord, all you works of His,
In all places of His dominion;
Bless the Lord, O my soul! (vv. 19–22)

David declares that God is sovereign over all, and this leads him to exhort all the angels to bless and obey the Lord—the same exhortation that all of us need, especially when we fail. For failure can be a powerful enemy to our morale, and rather than telling ourselves, like David, to bless and obey the Lord, we may begin saying, "Why try again? I'll never be able to pull things back together."

In the aftermath of failure, it is easy to forget that God's sovereignty means that He is in control and can bring good even out of our failures . . . if we continue to obey!

Succinct Lessons to Affect Tomorrow

We can glean at least two practical helps from our study of Psalm 103.

Control Your Expectations

We set ourselves up for failure when we stack our expectations too high. Be sure, as you set your goals, that you leave yourself some room to fail, to be human.

Leave the Results with God

Colossians 3:23 says, "Whatever you do, do your work heartily, as for the Lord rather than for men." We're to give life all we've got, but also to leave the results in God's hands. What may appear as a failure from our limited viewpoint may in fact be God's way of bringing about something good. Even Christ looked like a failure when He hung on the cross. But it was through that crushing experience that our very salvation was secured (Isa. 53).

Some Final Thoughts

The headline to that humorous newspaper article about Lucky read, "Look! There's ole Lucky in front of that Greyhound." He was about to flunk the final exam in his course on failure.

Many of us have experienced the crippling effects of being hit by failure. All kidding aside, it can be completely shattering, and many never recover. But even when we think we've been flattened by a bus, God is ready and waiting to pick us up and teach us to walk again. Failure can be a deterrent or an opportunity for growth. Which will it be for you?

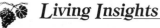 *Living Insights*   STUDY ONE

One man has called failure "the back door to success." Most of us would rather walk right in the front door; unfortunately, we frequently find the front door locked! To those in that predicament, Psalm 103 offers great encouragement.

- Let's gain a stronger grip on Psalm 103 by paraphrasing it, paragraph by paragraph. Many find that rewriting Scripture in their own words is a rewarding experience, an excellent vehicle for interacting personally with the text.

Verses 1–5

_____

_____

_____

_____

_____

Verses 6–14

_____

_____

_____

_____

_____

Verses 15–18

_____

_____

_____

Verses 19–22

_____

_____

_____

🍇 *Living Insights*   STUDY TWO

The study of Psalm 103 reveals five suggestions to put into practice after failure. Why not gather your family or close friends together
and discuss these applications. Encourage everyone to participate.
And don't forget to be a good listener.

- Think about failure in your life. Maybe it is in your past, or
  maybe you're in the midst of it. Let's talk about it.

1. Have you taken responsibility for your reactions? Why or why not? Is it difficult to do? Explain your situation.

_____

_____

_____

2. It's easy to blame others or yourself for failure. It boils down to a matter of focus. On what or whom are you focusing your failure? Why?

_____

_____

_____

3. Why is it important to be assured of God's complete acceptance? Do you have to "perform" in order to be acceptable to God? Feel free to bring in Scriptures that touch on this subject.

_____

_____

_____

4. How do you decide if you have failed—by looking at yourself, at others, or at God? What are the obvious dangers of comparing yourself with others? What are the subtle dangers?

_____

_____

_____

_____

5. How can failure be used to deepen your commitment to God? How has God used failure in your past to do that very work?

_____

_____

_____

_____

Chapter 3

GROWING THROUGH MISUNDERSTANDING

Psalm 140

Misunderstandings. They form lesions in our relationships that are often painfully difficult to heal. And there is no language, country, or vacation spot immune to them . . . no political asylum, big brother, or vaccine that can protect us from them. They occur between people who are hundreds of miles apart just as easily as between people who are only inches apart. Letters, phone calls, speeches, sermons, love notes, sometimes even our silence, all that we say and do are potential carriers of this blight that affects our relationships.

In his book *Communication: Key to Your Marriage,* Norman Wright points out six types of misunderstandings that may enter the bloodstream of any healthy conversation and immediately begin breaking it down.

> When you stop to think about all that's involved in getting your message across it's apparent why misunderstandings often occur. Communication specialists point out that when you talk with another person there are actually six messages that can come through.
>
> 1. What you mean to say.
> 2. What you actually say.
> 3. What the other person hears.
> 4. What the other person thinks he hears.
> 5. What the other person says about what you said.
> 6. What you think the other person said about what you said.[1]

Not exactly encouraging news. But there is someone who went through a serious bout with misunderstanding, and he has some encouraging words to share with us. First Samuel 18 records the onset of a misunderstanding in the life of David that lingered for years. For the next few minutes, let's examine this growing pain of David's and how he handled it.

1. H. Norman Wright, *Communication: Key to Your Marriage* (Glendale, Calif.: G/L Publications, 1974), p. 54.

The Background to Misunderstanding

One attempt at unraveling a misunderstanding goes like this:

> I know you believe you understand what you think I
> said, but I'm not sure you realize that what you heard
> is not what I meant.[2]

Let's hope there is an easier way of explaining the simple anatomy of misunderstandings!

In All Cases

Every misunderstanding develops in basically the same way. First, an innocent act, word, or motive is misinterpreted by someone who—based on this faulty perception—then becomes offended with the innocent person.

In David's Case

Every Sunday school child knows that David killed the giant Goliath. But what many teachers don't go on to tell us is that this led to a terrible misunderstanding between David and King Saul that would fester until the king's death.

When Saul and his warriors returned from conquering the Philistines, who had fled when David slew Goliath, they were met by an entourage of ecstatic women from all the cities of Israel.

> And it happened as they were coming, when David
> returned from killing the Philistine, that the women
> came out of all the cities of Israel, singing and dancing,
> to meet King Saul, with tambourines, with joy and
> with musical instruments. And the women sang as
> they played, and said,
> > "Saul has slain his thousands,
> > And David his ten thousands."
> > (1 Sam. 18:6–7)

When Saul heard the song, jealousy set in—he hungered for the honor that David was receiving.

> Then Saul became very angry, for this saying displeased
> him; and he said, "They have ascribed to David ten
> thousands, but to me they have ascribed thousands.
> Now what more can he have but the kingdom?" (v. 8)

---

2. Wright, *Communication: Key to Your Marriage*, p. 53.

Saul was more accurate than he knew; David had been anointed by the prophet Samuel to be the next king (16:1–13). But even so, he was not scheming to take the throne away from Saul. The king would never have a more devoted servant than David. And yet, because of Saul's own insecurities and lack of faith, Israel's great victory became a stumbling block in his relationship with David. As 18:9 tells us, "Saul looked at David with suspicion from that day on."

The Misery of Misunderstanding

Many Old Testament scholars believe that David's words in Psalm 140 arose from his long struggle with the king who misread his motives.[3] Let's listen in as he relates the emotions he feels—the same pains that accompany everyone's misunderstandings.

Vulnerability

David addresses the Lord like a man who feels highly exposed. "Rescue me, O Lord, . . . Preserve me" (v. 1), "Keep me, O Lord, . . . Preserve me" (v. 4).

We cannot protect ourselves from being misunderstood, and that leaves us feeling defenseless and vulnerable. It is often not even in our power to stop a misunderstanding once it has begun. And though our instincts tell us to defend ourselves, this usually only makes things worse. David is experiencing the painful reality that he is completely helpless to change the opinion of the one he has unwittingly offended.

Exaggeration

When Saul heard the women sing of David's "ten thousands," his mind immediately exaggerated David's victory as a step toward usurping the throne (1 Sam. 18:8). When people misunderstand, they often add to it with exaggerated imaginings that are allowed to run their darkest course. David knew this was happening with Saul.

> Rescue me, O Lord, from evil men;
> Preserve me from violent men,
> Who devise evil things in their hearts;
> They continually stir up wars. (Ps. 140:1–2)

Slight misunderstandings rarely stay that way. Until they are resolved, these distortions of truth can billow up into ominous storm fronts that block out any glimmering of reality.

---

3. See E. W. Hengstenberg, *Commentary on the Psalms* (Cherry Hill, N.J.: Mack Publishing Co., n.d.), vol. 3, p. 505.

Apprehension

Washington Irving said, "A sharp tongue is the only edge tool that grows keener with constant use."[4] And when it came to slandering David, Saul's tongue was razor sharp.

> They sharpen their tongues as a serpent;
> Poison of a viper is under their lips. (v. 3)

David was concerned about Saul infecting others with poisonous rumors, threats, and exaggerations that would turn them against him.

Suspicion

Saul convinced his followers that David was not to be trusted, which eventually forced David to live like a hunted animal.

> Keep me, O Lord, from the hands of the wicked;
> Preserve me from violent men,
> Who have purposed to trip up my feet.
> The proud have hidden a trap for me, and cords;
> They have spread a net by the wayside;
> They have set snares for me. (vv. 4–5)

Growth during Misunderstanding

But even through his pain, David goes on to remember things about the Lord that will enable him to grow during this misunderstanding.

First, David opens the door for growth by declaring his allegiance to the Lord. Rather than succumbing to the temptation to please his enemies, David entrusts himself to the One who does understand, who sees his motives and judges fairly.

> I said to the Lord, "Thou art my God;
> Give ear, O Lord, to the voice of my supplications."
> (v. 6)

Next, he reminds himself of the Lord's protection. David was defenseless against the kind of verbal spears that had been thrown in this battle of misunderstanding. So he counts on the Lord for his defense. David seeks the refuge of God as his shield.

> "O God the Lord, the strength of my salvation,
> Thou hast covered my head in the day of battle."
> (v. 7)

---

4. As quoted in *Bartlett's Familiar Quotations*, 14th ed., rev. and enl., ed. Emily Morison Beck (Boston, Mass.: Little, Brown and Co., 1968), p. 550.

Finally, David asks the Lord to do his fighting for him, to thwart the desires and devices of the wicked. David learned that he must trust the Lord to accomplish the victory in this battle, the same as he trusted Him to slay the giant Goliath and the rest of the Philistines.[5]

"Do not grant, O Lord, the desires of the wicked;
Do not promote his evil device, lest they be exalted.
As for the head of those who surround me,
May the mischief of their lips cover them.
May burning coals fall upon them;
May they be cast into the fire,
Into deep pits from which they cannot rise.
May a slanderer not be established in the earth;
May evil hunt the violent man speedily." (vv. 8–11)

The Assurance after Misunderstanding

As David concludes his psalm, we see his grasp on the divine perspective.

I know that the Lord will maintain the cause of the afflicted,
And justice for the poor.
Surely the righteous will give thanks to Thy name;
The upright will dwell in Thy presence. (vv. 12–13)

David sees that God will uphold the cause of all those who are suffering an injustice. We need never feel abandoned, even during those times when the whole world seems to be set on fire against us by a tongue fueled with misunderstanding.

That sense of God's support should inspire tremendous gratefulness . . . not only *after* our affliction, but *during* it, as well. By transferring our burdens to Him, we can know the fullness of joy that comes from dwelling in His presence (Ps. 16:11).

As we grow in the Lord, all of us will encounter misunderstandings. Like David, when he slew Goliath, some of our greatest words and deeds done in pure faith will be attributed to evil motives.

The twenty-sixth president of the United States, Theodore Roosevelt, knew what it was like to be misunderstood. And he left behind these encouraging words:

It is not the critic who counts; not the man who points out how the strong man stumbles or where the

5. David did experience God's protection, just as he had prayed. See 1 Samuel 18:10–11.

19

doer of deeds could have done them better. The credit belongs to the man who is actually in the arena, whose face is marred by dust and sweat and blood; who strives valiantly; who errs, and comes short again and again, because there is no effort without error and short-coming; but who does actually try to do the deeds; who knows the great enthusiasms, the great devotions, who spends himself in a worthy cause; who at the best knows in the end the triumph of high achievement, and who at the worst, if he fails, at least fails while daring greatly, so that his place shall never be with those cold and timid souls who know neither victory nor defeat.[6]

 ## Living Insights STUDY ONE

So often misunderstanding is produced through what we say. Psalm 140 speaks of tongues that are as sharp as those of serpents. The same idea is expanded in the New Testament passage of James 3.

- Read Psalm 140:3, 9, and 11, and James 3:1–12 together. As you read these two passages, certain similarities will become apparent. Record your observations in the space provided, giving the verse or verses first.

_____

_____

_____

_____

_____

In light of your observations, read Ephesians 4:29. Then answer the question, Are there areas in my life where I am spreading the poison of misunderstanding rather than building up through edification?

Family _____

Friends _____

6. Theodore Roosevelt, from the speech "Citizen in a Republic," given at the Sorbonne, Paris, France, April 23, 1910, as quoted in *The Man in the Arena*, ed. John Allen Gable (Oyster Books, N.Y.: Theodore Roosevelt Association, 1987), p. 54.

People in Authority _____

My Enemies _____

People Different from Me _____

Other Relationships _____

![] *Living Insights* STUDY TWO

It's possible to learn from this message from either side of a misunderstanding. Right now you could be one who is misunderstood . . . or you could be one who has misunderstood another.

- Are you misunderstood? By whom? Have you found yourself vulnerable to others' uncalled-for reactions? Have your words or actions been exaggerated or misinterpreted? Has this made you feel apprehensive? Take a few minutes to carefully think through and jot down some practical truths this lesson has taught you.

_____

_____

_____

_____

_____

- Is it possible that you haven't given someone a fair shake? Have you jumped to conclusions, rather than carefully considering alternative meanings to what have seemed to be hurtful words or actions? Spend a few minutes developing a plan to help rectify the situation.

_____

_____

_____

_____

_____

Chapter 4

GROWING THROUGH LOSS
Job 1–2

*B*ridge to Terabithia is a story of a special friendship between a young boy and girl. Although from different backgrounds, their hearts were knit together in a secret kingdom of their own creation called Terabithia. Like all of us, they both longed for a friend that "you did everything with and told everything to."[1] And like a lucky few of us, they found it.

One day, the rope that swung them over a creek from their ordinary world to the shores of their enchanted world broke. The eleven-year-old queen of Terabithia drowned—and Jesse, her king, had to learn how to continue growing through his loss.

The story of Terabithia grew out of an event in real life; the author's eight-year-old son lost his best friend when she was struck by lightning. Katherine Paterson shares about her son's subsequent struggle to grow through this loss in a later book, *Gates of Excellence*, saying,

> He is not fully healed. Perhaps he will never be, and I am beginning to believe that this is right. How many people in their whole lifetimes have a friend who is to them what Lisa was to David? When you have had such a gift, should you ever forget it? Of course he will forget a little. Even now he is making other friendships. His life will go on, though hers could not. And selfishly I want his pain to ease. But how can I say that I want him to "get over it," as though having loved and been loved were some sort of disease? I want the joy of knowing Lisa and the sorrow of losing her to be a part of him and to shape him into growing levels of caring and understanding, perhaps as an artist, but certainly as a person.[2]

1. Katherine Paterson, *Gates of Excellence* (New York, N.Y.: Elsevier-Dutton Publishing Co., 1981), p. 96.

2. Paterson, *Gates of Excellence*, pp. 97–98.

Maybe you, too, know what it's like to have your life molded by the pressure and pain of loss. If so, there's someone you should meet. Job. Meet him in the brutal ring of suffering recorded in the first two chapters of his book—there he gets hit with incredible losses not unlike some of our own. Perhaps there with Job, in the deep intimacy of shared hurt, we can learn something that will show us how to grow through loss.

Three Key Facts about Experiencing Loss

To better understand and appreciate our own reaction to loss, as well as Job's, we first need to examine three key facts.

Categories of Loss

When we speak of loss, we can run through a gamut of meanings from trivial to serious, from losing our balance or courage to losing our will to live or even our souls (Mark 8:36). So to help focus our attention, let's zero in on two major categories.

First is the loss of significant individuals. At one time or another, all of us will be baptized into this experience either by death or by distance. Death may administer its last rites through illness, an accident, old age, war, or miscarriage. Distance may separate no less brutally through misunderstandings, divorce, or the waning intimacy of a friend who has moved away.

Second is the loss of personal necessities or benefits. Maybe you've walked through the charcoaled ruins of a burned home, or felt the violation of a burglary, or gone through the grief of letting a longtime dream die. Perhaps you've been hit with sudden unemployment or had the loss of a business drain the financial resources of a lifetime.

The losses may be different between the two categories, but the feelings share the same intensity.

Reactions to Loss

The characteristics of grief are probably familiar to most of us. First there is shock and panic, followed by denial, which eventually yields to anger and disillusionment. Then comes depression, and finally a resolution of some sort.

Now on the surface, there appear to be as many different resolutions to grief as there are people. Yet underneath, basically only two kinds are reflected, the common and the rare.

23

The *common resolution* includes lifelong depression, resentment, and bitterness. The *rare resolution*, however, involves the uncharacteristic response of acceptance. Accepting the loss—after we walk down the long, dark corridors of grief—opens the door for submission, which then leads to growth.

Grieving is a part of the normal human experience, a part that even Jesus shared (John 11:35), and shouldn't be viewed as unspiritual. So how can we acknowledge our grief, yet move through it with measured steps toward growth and maturity, instead of dissolving into lifelong bitterness and resentment?

It's a matter of perspective.

Perspectives on Loss

It is our perspective that will determine whether our reaction to loss will be common or rare. If our perspective is strictly horizontal, focused on the things of this world, then we cannot escape mere hopeless grief. If, however, our focus is vertical, fixed on the Lord, then we will be able to look beyond the anguish and the disappointment to experience hope and growth.

Job: A Classic Case Study

With these key facts in mind, as well as our own experiences of loss, let's enter into Job's world by first taking the time to see and possibly feel what Job lost, then seeing what his response can teach us.

What He Had

Beginning in Job 1:1, we are given a personal inventory of Job's spiritual and material wealth. At the top of that list is Job's own personal character. There's nothing that suggests he pursued spiritual things because he had the title of "full-time minister" to live up to. Instead, he was an ordinary person whose godly reputation came not from a title, but from a genuine, committed walk with God.

The list continues with the blessings of children, livestock, and many servants. Laid out all at once on one-dimensional paper, it is easy to think this is how it always must have been for Job. We forget that he, too, went through the trials of raising ten children, building a successful business, and cultivating a love for God in the midst of it all. Remembering this may help us identify with Job better as we turn our attention from what he possessed to what he lost.

What He Lost

Satan was sure that Job followed God only because of His blessings, and that if they were taken away, Job's faith in God would dissolve. And so to prove His servant, God allowed the growing pain of loss to be brought upon Job.[3]

> Now it happened on the day when his sons and his daughters were eating and drinking wine in their oldest brother's house, that a messenger came to Job and said, "The oxen were plowing and the donkeys feeding beside them, and the Sabeans attacked and took them. They also slew the servants with the edge of the sword, and I alone have escaped to tell you." While he was still speaking, another also came and said, "The fire of God fell from heaven and burned up the sheep and the servants and consumed them, and I alone have escaped to tell you." While he was still speaking, another also came and said, "The Chaldeans formed three bands and made a raid on the camels and took them and slew the servants with the edge of the sword; and I alone have escaped to tell you." While he was still speaking, another also came and said, "Your sons and your daughters were eating and drinking wine in their oldest brother's house, and behold, a great wind came from across the wilderness and struck the four corners of the house, and it fell on the young people and they died; and I alone have escaped to tell you." (Job 1:13–19)

Everything that Job had worked and prayed for over the years was brutally torn out of his life in an instant.

How It Happened

Satan didn't send up any warning flags so that Job could prepare himself. He just came up behind Job and hit him with all the meanness and power he could put into a blow. It resulted in the utter devastation of Job's wealth and family from which nothing could be recovered.

How He Reacted

Job's reaction to having everything stripped away from him was pretty disappointing . . . for Satan.

> Then Job arose and tore his robe and shaved his head, and he fell to the ground and worshiped. (v. 20)

---

3. All losses are not necessarily because of some wrong. In Job's case, it was his blameless character and faith, not sin, that prompted his being tested by grievous losses.

Job was able to respond in worship because he had never taken possession of the blessings God had given him. He had never built up the unrealistic expectation that God's blessings were his to keep for the rest of his life. Job recognized that he was only a steward of God's blessings, not the owner, and that God can do with His possessions as He pleases. When God allowed all that He had given Job to be taken away, it served only to remind Job of God's sovereign reign over all things and His right to be worshiped.

> And he said,
> > "Naked I came from my mother's womb,
> > And naked I shall return there.
> > The Lord gave and the Lord has taken
> > > away.
> > Blessed be the name of the Lord."
> Through all this Job did not sin nor did he blame God.
> (vv. 21–22)

Right off, in round one, Job's response almost knocked Satan out for the full count. But Satan got back up on his feet and was granted a second round from the Lord to try to bring Job's faith to its knees.

> Then Satan went out from the presence of the Lord, and smote Job with sore boils from the sole of his foot to the crown of his head.[4] And he took a potsherd to scrape himself while he was sitting among the ashes. (2:7–8)

Despite his miserable physical condition and the emotional grief brought on by his losses, especially that of his children, Job continued to respond by trusting in God. But somewhere in the midst of all this, Job's wife had already decided to throw in the towel and advised Job to do the same.

> Then his wife said to him, "Do you still hold fast your integrity? Curse God and die!" (v. 9)

---

4. One commentary says that this is most likely elephantiasis, "so called because the limbs become jointless lumps like elephants' legs. . . . The disease begins with the rising of tubercular boils, and at length resembles a cancer spreading itself over the whole body, by which the body is so affected, that some of the limbs fall completely away. Scraping with a potsherd will not only relieve the intolerable itching of the skin, but also remove the matter." C. F. Keil and F. Delitzsch, *Commentary on the Old Testament* (reprint, Grand Rapids, Mich.: William B. Eerdmans Publishing Co., 1978), vol. 4, pp. 69–70.

No one needs to wonder which of the two responses, common or rare, she had chosen. Her shock had turned into anger, which was now settling into a deep disillusionment, garnered with bitterness. She had taken God's gifts and turned them into her rights—the right to a big family, money, prestige—and now she wants her husband to share her bitterness. Instead, Job gives her some counsel from the rare perspective.

> But he said to her, "You speak as one of the foolish women speaks. Shall we indeed accept good from God and not accept adversity?" In all this Job did not sin with his lips. (v. 10)

Lessons from a Seasoned Sufferer

As we leave Job and turn to face the painful losses in our own lives, let's remember three important lessons.

Our major goal in life is not to be happy or satisfied, but to glorify God (Job 5:17–21).

In his book *Effective Biblical Counseling*, Larry Crabb points out that

> many of us place top priority not on becoming Christ like in the middle of our problems but on finding happiness. . . . I must firmly and consciously by an act of my will reject the goal of becoming happy and adopt the goal of becoming more like the Lord. The result will be happiness for me as I learn to dwell at God's right hand in fellowship with Christ.[5]

This cuts across the grain with the modern mind-set, which says happiness is our inalienable right. God's goal, however, is not that we should never experience trials, but that by them we should be conformed to His image and bring Him glory.

The path of obedience is marked by times of loss and suffering (Job 23:8–14).

Job concludes this passage of Scripture by saying, "For He performs what is appointed for me, And many such decrees are with Him" (v. 14). Our paths will be marked with losses and sufferings, which are allowed by God in order to bring glory to Himself. The same as they were for Jesus who, "although He was a Son, He learned obedience from the things which He suffered" (Heb. 5:8).

5. Lawrence J. Crabb, Jr., *Effective Biblical Counseling* (Grand Rapids, Mich.: Zondervan Publishing House, 1977), p. 20.

What is considered loss now often leads to gain later
(Job 42:10–17).

The purpose of Job's losses was not simply so that the Lord could come back later and give him great blessings, even though this was done. The greatest gain for Job, as for all who suffer a loss and continue trusting God, was in glorifying God and knowing Him even more deeply than before.

> But whatever things were gain to me, those things I have counted as loss for the sake of Christ. More than that, I count all things to be loss in view of the surpassing value of knowing Christ Jesus my Lord, for whom I have suffered the loss of all things, and count them but rubbish in order that I may gain Christ. (Phil. 3:7–8)

 Living Insights _____ STUDY ONE

Job is a classic study in loss. He's a great example of the principle "Perspective determines growth." By examining select portions of the book of Job, we can find timeless principles for growing through loss.

- Read the following Scriptures carefully, and based on your observations, put into writing principles of growth that you can apply, either today or in the future.

Job 1:20–22 _____

_____

_____

Job 2:7–10 _____

_____

_____

Job 23:8–14 _____

_____

_____

Job 42:10–17 _____

_____

_____

**Living Insights**

Loss . . . no one likes to think about it, but all of us go through it. The story of Job is one of sharp penetration. Its piercing message needs to be further personalized.

- Use this time to write a journal entry, using the space provided. Describe your feelings during a time of loss—perhaps of a family member, job, dream, health, or security. What was your perspective: horizontal or vertical? What was your reaction: common or rare? How could God have been glorified through this loss? Record your honest, open feelings.

_____

_____

_____

_____

_____

_____

_____

_____

_____

_____

_____

_____

_____

_____

_____

_____

_____

_____

Chapter 5

GROWING THROUGH MISTAKES

Psalm 31, Selected Scripture

M istakes. They can be as simple as forgetting to turn off the hall light or as serious as letting the grease on the stove get too hot. The difference is that while one may cost you only a few extra cents, the other may cost you everything you own.

Today the word *mistake* has many different meanings. Some see it as being synonymous with sin. Others rename their mistakes *experience* or, like many celebrities, put them all together in a book and call them memoirs. According to Webster, however, a mistake is "a wrong action or statement proceeding from faulty judgment, inadequate knowledge, or inattention."[1]

Mistakes, then, are not out-and-out rebellion, deception, or willful disobedience. Those things are clearly sin. What we want to focus on in this lesson are those honest mistakes we're prone to make that can start another growing pain.

Categories and Examples of Mistakes

In the Scriptures we can see at least five kinds of mistakes and some of the things that lead up to them.

Panic-prompted Mistakes

Panic-prompted mistakes are the ones we make out of fear, hurry, or worry. Like the one Abraham made, recorded for us in Genesis 12. In verses 1–3, God had promised to give Abraham land, to make him a great nation, and to bestow His continued blessing on Abraham's life. But when a famine struck, Abraham panicked, and instead of relying on God, packed his bags and headed for Egypt— well-known enemy territory (v. 10). Oftentimes, it's our panic-prompted mistakes that put us into situations which can lead to sin. And that is exactly what happened to Abraham.

> And it came about when he came near to Egypt, that he said to Sarai his wife, "See now, I know that you

---

1. *Webster's Ninth New Collegiate Dictionary*, see "mistake."

are a beautiful woman; and it will come about when the Egyptians see you, that they will say, 'This is his wife'; and they will kill me, but they will let you live. Please say that you are my sister so that it may go well with me because of you, and that I may live on account of you." (vv. 11–13)

With that, Abraham crossed the line between making a mistake and outright sinning. His mistake backed him into telling a lie.

Well-Intentioned Mistakes

Like all genuine mistakes, well-intentioned ones stem from trying to do right, but at the wrong time or in the wrong way. Exodus 2 records just such a mistake in Moses' life.

> Now it came about in those days, when Moses had grown up, that he went out to his brethren and looked on their hard labors; and he saw an Egyptian beating a Hebrew, one of his brethren. So he looked this way and that, and when he saw there was no one around, he struck down the Egyptian and hid him in the sand. (vv. 11–12)

Moses' desire to defend his Hebrew brother was right, well-intentioned. But he relied on his own power to deliver the Hebrew from the Egyptian, rather than on the power of God, and this led to the sin of murder.

Negligent Mistakes

Mistakes of negligence result from laziness, lack of discipline, or inconsistency. In Scripture they're often associated with fathers. And one father who made this mistake was David. First Kings 1 tells the story. In it, David is old and has had many wives, one of which had given him a son named Adonijah.

> Now Adonijah the son of Haggith exalted himself, saying, "I will be king." So he prepared for himself chariots and horsemen with fifty men to run before him. And his father had never crossed him at any time by asking, "Why have you done so?" And he was also a very handsome man; and he was born after Absalom. (vv. 5–6)

We can see from this passage that David had never provided the discipline his son needed. As a result, Adonijah's childhood rebellion grew into a plan to take the throne from his father.[2]

Unrestrained-Curiosity Mistakes

Curiosity is a very creative and important part of our lives. But if not restrained, it can often lead to trouble—sometimes in areas related to the demonic or sensational.

First Samuel 28 records King Saul's unrestrained curiosity about the outcome of a battle, which led him to seek the counsel of a spiritist medium. The Philistines had gathered for war against Israel, and Saul's "heart trembled greatly" at the sight of them (v. 5). He had lost his confidence; Samuel, his spiritual adviser, had died; and God was not answering any of his inquiries. Finally, he turned to a spiritist.

> Then Saul said to his servants, "Seek for me a woman who is a medium, that I may go to her and inquire of her." (v. 7a)

Wholesome curiosity is a helpful key that has unlocked many a door in our understanding of the world. Unrestrained curiosity is a different key, however—a key to a Pandora's box of evils that is best left unopened.

Blind-Spot Mistakes

Blind-spot mistakes are the ones we commit because of ignorance, habit, parental influence, or some character weakness. We're often not even aware of making them!

Acts 15:36–41 records an example of this kind of mistake in the story of a conflict between two godly men, Paul and Barnabas. When they were preparing for their second missionary journey together, Barnabas wanted to take young John Mark along. But because he had deserted them on the first missionary journey, Paul was against it. In Paul's mind, John Mark's faith was too shallow, too weak to be of help to them. Paul had a blind spot when it came to immature faith in other people. And so he made a mistake in judgment—one he came to recognize later in his ministry (see 2 Tim. 4:11).

---

2. David made this same mistake when his son Amnon raped his half sister Tamar. The Scriptures record that David became very angry (2 Sam. 13:21), but did nothing about it. Amnon was later killed by another of David's sons, Absalom, Tamar's full brother. Again David did nothing about it, and when Absalom reached maturity, he, like Adonijah, caused David a lot of misery.

Of all our mistakes, this kind is usually the most difficult for us to discern. We want to rationalize the rightness of our blind-spot mistakes time and time again, rather than admit that we may have blown it.

Perspective on Mistakes

At the time David penned Psalm 31, it appears he was broken, disappointed in himself, possibly under the gun from recent mistakes, discouraged. On the heels of these bad mistakes, David turned to the Lord for the comfort and encouragement that only He can give. As we read his words, we can find some insight into how God responds to our mistakes.

How He Views Us When We Make Mistakes

David tells us that God views us realistically and thoroughly.

> I will rejoice and be glad in Thy lovingkindness,
> Because Thou hast seen my affliction;
> Thou hast known the troubles of my soul. (v. 7)

David rejoices because God sees us where we are, even in the messes that our mistakes have made. Nothing about our circumstances, our bad habits, or how we were raised is hidden from Him. God also knows the dark sides of our souls. He knows our fears, doubts, shame; He probes down inside us and knows us for who we really are (see also Ps. 139).

How He Treats Us When We Make Mistakes

There is a deep-seated tug-of-war in all of us to be fully known and yet to keep parts of ourselves hidden from view. If God sees us realistically and thoroughly, our next question would logically be, How will He treat us? Verse 8 calms our anxiety.

> And Thou hast not given me over into the hand of
> the enemy. (v. 8a)

What's the one thing we fear most when our mistakes are exposed? Rejection. But David declares that God doesn't reject us. The flow of His love is not regulated by the amount or size of our mistakes.

Next, David declares that God gives us space to learn from our mistakes.

> Thou hast set my feet in a large place. (v. 8b)

God doesn't crowd in and take control of our lives every time we're about to make a mistake. Instead, He gives us room to grow and learn.

How He instructs Us When We Make Mistakes

First, He instructs us in a context of trust, not suspicion.

> But as for me, I trust in Thee, O Lord,
> I say, "Thou art my God." (v. 14)

God never gets fed up with us, even after we've come to Him with the same mistake for the hundredth time. We can always trust Him to help us.

Second, God instructs us in *all* of life, not just the pleasant times.

> My times are in Thy hand. (v. 15a)

Even when we are ashamed, embarrassed, humiliated, or failing, He will meet us with love and gentle instruction.

Third, He instructs us privately, not publicly.

> How great is Thy goodness,
> Which Thou hast stored up for those who fear Thee,
> Which Thou hast wrought for those who take refuge
>   in Thee,
> Before the sons of men!
> Thou dost hide them in the secret place of Thy pres-
>   ence from the conspiracies of man;
> Thou dost keep them secretly in a shelter from the
>   strife of tongues.
> (vv. 19–20)

The best lessons are taught when we are alone, when the secret chambers of our hearts are open to hearing God's wisdom.

Insight about Mistakes

The next time you sense you're about to make a mistake, try checking three things: your motive, your moment, and your method. However, when you do make a mistake, keep in mind these comforting thoughts. First, *I'm human.* As simple as that may sound, it is often the very thing we need to be reminded of when we start punishing ourselves for not being perfect. Second, *Through this I have learned* _____ (fill in the blank). Third, remember, *I will recover.* As David said, as he ended his psalm,

> Be strong, and let your heart take courage,
> All you who hope in the Lord.
> (v. 24)

🍇 *Living Insights*

We often think of characters in the Bible as bigger than life. Certainly they couldn't make mistakes, right? Wrong! As this study revealed, their mistakes are accurately recorded in the Old and New Testaments.

- Are you prone toward one category of mistake? Which one is it? Why not take a biblical character who illustrates that particular type and study the related account in further detail. Write down words or phrases that are especially meaningful to you. Perhaps they'll include emotions that remind you of your feelings during times of mistakes.

Categories	Examples
☐ Panic-prompted Mistakes	Abraham (Gen. 12:1–13)
☐ Well-Intentioned Mistakes	Moses (Exod. 2:11–12)
☐ Negligent Mistakes	David (1 Kings 1:5–6)
☐ Unrestrained-Curiosity Mistakes	Saul (1 Sam. 28)
☐ Blind-Spot Mistakes	Paul (Acts 15:36–41)

_____

_____

_____

_____

_____

🍇 *Living Insights*

We all make mistakes. Perhaps we need to design a pencil suited more to our needs . . . one-quarter inch of pencil and six inches of eraser! Could you use such an invention? Blunders are a sign of our humanity.

- In the space provided on the next page, write out the category of mistake you are prone to make most often. Then write out the principles from the study that will be most helpful in dealing with this kind of mistake.

My Mistake Category: _____

_____

_____

_____

_____

_____

_____

_____

_____

_____

_____

_____

Chapter 6
GROWING THROUGH WEAKNESS
Psalm 46

Sometimes trials come at us with the full battle fury and tearing sword of one of Homer's mighty warriors in *The Iliad*. They charge into the rank and file of our lives and wreak havoc, like Achilleus of the swift feet, who charged into the ranks of the Trojans like a wild boar, wielding sword and spear and despoiling his vanquished of their armor. Terrible plumed helmuts, massive gilded shields, iron corselets, bronzed leg greaves—all were torn away for booty and to shame, leaving behind only frail and vulnerable bodies.

Many of us know what it is like to feel frail and vulnerable. To have a trial, like Achilleus, knock us down and, with its heavy foot on our necks, strip away our jobs, money, achievements—the kind of armor we don today to hide our weaknesses and make us feel stronger. But no matter how impenetrable our armor seems, it cannot protect us from the piercing truth . . . we're only human. Being sinful, we fail. Being prone to sickness, we hurt. Being mortal, we ultimately die. Pressure wears on us. Anxiety gives us ulcers. People intimidate us. Criticism offends us. Disease scares us. Death haunts us.

Yet it is our weakness that opens the door to strength. Not a door we walk through proudly with heads held high, but one through which we must stoop to enter. It's the same door the apostle Paul often passed through in order to exchange his weakness for God's strength. Let's pause for just a moment in Paul's autobiographical book of 2 Corinthians to hear his own testimony of growing through weakness.

Paul's Testimony to Weakness

In 2 Corinthians Paul periodically unveils those things that have led to his growth. One very surprising list of such things is found in chapter 11, verses 23–30.

> . . . in far more imprisonments, beaten times without number, often in danger of death. Five times I received from the Jews thirty-nine lashes. Three times I was beaten with rods, once I was stoned, three times I was

shipwrecked, a night and a day I have spent in the deep. I have been on frequent journeys, in dangers from rivers, dangers from robbers, dangers from my countrymen, dangers from the Gentiles, dangers in the city, dangers in the wilderness, dangers on the sea, dangers among false brethren; I have been in labor and hardship, through many sleepless nights, in hunger and thirst, often without food, in cold and exposure. Apart from such external things, there is the daily pressure upon me of concern for all the churches. Who is weak without my being weak? Who is led into sin without my intense concern? If I have to boast, I will boast of what pertains to my weakness.

You might expect Paul to boast about the churches he founded or the influence he had or his Damascus road encounter with Christ. But instead, he would rather boast of his weaknesses. Why? He pulls back the veil on the answer to this question in 12:8–10. Beginning in verse 7, Paul mentions the nagging "thorn in the flesh" that humbled him.

And because of the surpassing greatness of the revelations, for this reason, to keep me from exalting myself, there was given me a thorn in the flesh, a messenger of Satan to buffet me—to keep me from exalting myself! Concerning this I entreated the Lord three times that it might depart from me. And He has said to me, "My grace is sufficient for you, for power is perfected in weakness." Most gladly, therefore, I will rather boast about my weaknesses, that the power of Christ may dwell in me. Therefore I am well content with weaknesses, with insults, with distresses, with persecutions, with difficulties, for Christ's sake; for when I am weak, then I am strong.

Paul learned that being weak opened the door for God's power to be released and brought to fulfillment in his life.

It is interesting to think about what Paul's stress rating would be according to the study done by Dr. Thomas H. Holmes and his colleagues at the University of Washington.

They came to the conclusion that an accumulation of 200 or more "life change units" in any year may mean more disruption than an individual can stand. On their scale, death of spouse equals 100 units, divorce equals 73 units, and Christmas equals 12 units![1]

From a strictly human viewpoint, they felt no person *in their own strength* could handle stresses totaling two hundred or more life change units in one year. Paul's stress in any given year must have rated in the thousands. But because he was willing to admit his weakness, God was able to be strong through him.

An Overview of Psalm 46

The Hebrew title of the book of Psalms means "songs sung with a stringed instrument." Psalm 46 was composed by the sons of Korah, during a time of trouble. It is a song about growing through weakness, which Paul may have sung quite frequently! Before we begin our look into the words of this song, let's briefly consider some details that will help open it up for us.

Set to Alamoth

The word *Alamoth* is the plural of the Hebrew word *almah*, meaning "young maiden, young woman." So some have concluded that this song was to be sung by a women's choir. However, throughout the whole Old Testament, no such choir is mentioned. The only other place *alamoth* occurs is in 1 Chronicles 15, where the Levites have been given the task of choosing among themselves who would sing and play instruments for Israel. In verse 20, we see that the men were to have their harps tuned to *alamoth*, a maiden-like tone. Apparently, the sons of Korah wanted the timbre of Psalm 46 to possess a quality produced by high-pitched instruments that would long be remembered.

A Repetitious Reminder

Psalm 46 contains a phrase that is sung twice, presumably so that its truth will linger in the listener's mind: "The Lord of hosts is with us; / The God of Jacob is our stronghold" (vv. 7, 11).

Selah

An interesting notation is inserted three times down the right margin of Psalm 46—the word *selah.* Throughout the book of Psalms, this word appears more than seventy times. Yet nobody knows for sure what this notation means. It probably served as a musical reminder, indicating a pause for silence or emphasis, or perhaps a crescendo in volume.

1. Stuart Briscoe, *What Works When Life Doesn't* (Wheaton, Ill.: SP Publications, Victor Books, 1976), p. 126.

Theme: *God Is Our Refuge in Times of Stress and Weakness*

The most important observation to note is the theme, which is revealed in verse 1. Paraphrased, it means "God is our immediate help when we are in a tight squeeze." The word *trouble* in Hebrew means "to be restricted, to be tied up in a narrow, cramped place." The psalmists were feeling pressed into a corner, under stress; their weaknesses were being exposed. And at those times, God is a "refuge and strength" (v. 1).

The Situations of Life

Many of life's circumstances threaten to strip away the things we rely on for strength. In each of the three sections of Psalm 46 (verses 1–3, 4–7, and 8–11), a difficult situation that preys upon our weakness is presented, accompanied by a response.

Situation: Nature in Upheaval

Every year thousands lose their homes, possessions, and even their lives in mud slides, earthquakes, tornadoes, fires, floods, and other upheavals in nature. In a matter of minutes, everything we have accumulated for comfort and security can be burned, buried, or broken. But this is not a modern phenomenon.

> God is our refuge and strength,
> A very present help in trouble.
> Therefore we will not fear, though the earth should change,
> And though the mountains slip into the heart of the sea;
> Though its waters roar and foam,
> Though the mountains quake at its swelling pride.
> (vv. 1–3)

Even though surrounded by natural disasters, the psalmists assert that they "will not fear" (v. 2). By trusting in God as their refuge and strength, they have had their weakness of anxiety replaced by His peaceful calm.[2]

Situation: Civil Disturbance

Next, the scene shifts from threats from nature to threats from people. Verses 4–7 picture nations and kingdoms rising up for war against Jerusalem, "the city of God."

---

2. For further study on assurance, see Joshua 1:9; Psalm 27:1, 91:1–2 and 5–10; Isaiah 41:10; 2 Timothy 1:7; 1 Peter 5:6–7.

There is a river whose streams make glad the city of God,
The holy dwelling places of the Most High.
God is in the midst of her, she will not be moved;
God will help her when morning dawns.
The nations made an uproar, the kingdoms tottered;
He raised His voice, the earth melted.
The Lord of hosts is with us;
The God of Jacob is our stronghold.

The sons of Korah declare they "will not be moved" (v. 5). The word *moved* comes from the Hebrew word that means "to totter or to shake in order to bring down." Despite the raging peoples who've come against them, Jerusalem's reaction is one of stability, because "God is in the midst of her" (v. 5).

Situation: The Aftermath of the Battle

The final section moves us into that difficult realm of stress that usually follows a test.

Come, behold the works of the Lord,
Who has wrought desolations in the earth.
He makes wars to cease to the end of the earth;
He breaks the bow and cuts the spear in two;
He burns the chariots with fire.
"Cease striving and know that I am God;
I will be exalted among the nations, I will be exalted
    in the earth."
The Lord of hosts is with us;
The God of Jacob is our stronghold. (vv. 8–11)

In the aftermath of a battle, people can be plagued with all kinds of feelings. Fatigue, depression, anxiety, remorse, guilt . . . to name just a few. Yet, according to God's directive, the Israelites were to cease striving, *raphah*, "relax!" Stop striving in your weaknesses and make yourself sit down and still your heart and mind so you can know the Lord is God.

The Strength of God

Sooner or later, we will all have trials land on our shores to test the strength of our inner fortitude. Even now one may be pressing in on you. With its scourge of difficulties, it is testing your every defense, looking for a weakness to exploit. By now it may have already beaten down your shield, knocked away your sword, and pinned you down, helpless and weak. Remember that there is one suit of armor that no trial can pierce or strip away—God's strength.

To clothe ourselves with the divine armor of God's strength, let's remember three things. First, *His strength is immediately available.* Whether you are in times of peace or in the thick of battle, it is never too late to receive His strength. He is "a very present help in trouble" (v. 1). Second, *His power is overpowering.* There is no weakness that He cannot stretch the tent of His power to cover. Third, *God's power is sufficient without our help.* He only wants us to be willing, like Paul, to admit our weakness and rely on Him to provide the strength we need.

> Most gladly, therefore, I will rather boast about my weaknesses, that the power of Christ may dwell in me. (2 Cor. 12:9b).

 ## *Living Insights*

STUDY ONE

"Therefore I am well content with weaknesses, with insults, with distresses, with persecutions, with difficulties, for Christ's sake; for when I am weak, then I am strong" (2 Cor. 12:10). In this verse, the apostle Paul sums up weakness and its value in our lives.

- Let's conduct a Scripture search. Using a Bible concordance (a separate volume or the one in the back of your Bible), look up the word *weakness.* Record your observations regarding several uses of the word.

Weakness

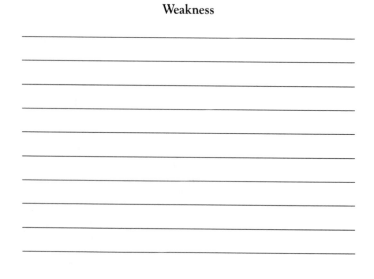

Have you given serious thought to weakness in your life? Time spent in consideration of this concept would be time well used.

- As you look at the following questions, seek to answer each one objectively. You may want to discuss them with a close friend in order to gain even greater insights.

Where am I weak? _____

_____

_____

_____

_____

What part does God play in dealing with weakness? _____

_____

_____

_____

_____

Am I growing through weakness? _____ How do I know? _____

_____

_____

_____

_____

Am I content in weakness? _____ How do I know? _____

_____

_____

_____

_____

Chapter 7

GROWING THROUGH MONOTONY

Psalm 90

Sisyphus was a popular figure of Greek mythology, known for being a trickster and master thief. Unfortunately, he made the egregious mistake of cheating Death—and his punishment was severe.

> The cunning king of Corinth . . . was punished in Hades by repeatedly having to roll a huge stone up a hill only to have it always roll down again as soon as he had brought it to the summit.[1]

Up and down, up and down, up and down, . . . *forever.*

Many of us feel as if we can relate to Sisyphus—trapped in a life of meaningless tasks. We are, as Thoreau said, leading "lives of quiet desperation,"[2] because we don't sense any purpose in our activities. Monotony has sucked out the vitality from the well-worn paths and routines of our lives. There are no risks, no unexpected changes, no highs or lows. Only the tedium of repetitious rock-pushing.

Although Psalm 90 addresses the subject of monotony in only an indirect way, there are some practical principles we can borrow from it to ease our growing pain of monotony.

Observing the Psalm

Before we hike into the interior of the psalm, it would help if we first learned something of its history, unique features, and general boundaries.

Writer

According to the superscription, this psalm has its roots in the fertile soil of Moses' life. The same Moses whom many imagine spent his life leaping from one exciting mountaintop experience to the next. Probably the last person you would feel comfortable talking to about your struggles with monotony. "No way he could relate,"

---

1. *The New Encyclopaedia Britannica,* 15th edition, see "Sisyphus."

2. Henry David Thoreau, *Thoreau: Walden and Other Writings,* ed. Joseph Wood Krutch (New York, N.Y.: Bantam Books, 1971), p. 111.

we think. But in between those peaks there were some very monotonous valleys, and Moses spent more time than many of us realize traversing them.

Some of you are probably thinking, "But wasn't Moses raised by one of Pharoah's daughters with all the riches and variety of Egypt at his disposal? What would he know of monotony?" Remember that when Moses fled from the lively high courts of Egypt he ended up down in the Midian desert keeping company with a herd of sheep. For forty years—14,400 days—Moses' life was shared with an animal that hates surprises and loves sameness.

"Yes, but then there was the burning bush, the miracles in Egypt, the Exodus!" It's true, Moses did experience all that. But only for a relatively brief time in his life. Then he came down into another wearisome "valley." This time to spend the last forty years of his life wandering aimlessly with the rest of the Israelites, who were afraid to possess the land God had given them. Same terrain, same people, same complaints, same heat, same stultifying dust. Okay, who wants to be first to compare monotony stories with Moses?

Style

The style of Moses' psalm is a prayer. The kind of prayer that comes from a man who finds himself trapped in humdrum demands and tedious daily tasks.

Outline

Moses' prayer breaks easily into two sections. In verses 1–2, Moses gives his full attention to the Lord and His majesty. Then in verses 3–17 he takes on the meaninglessness of life and man's monotony. It would also be helpful to note Moses' subtle shift from speaking about mankind in general ("they" in verses 3–6) to using more personal terms ("we" in verses 7–17).

Breaking the Spell

Oftentimes the sing-song sameness of monotonous routines has a mesmerizing effect on our spirits. Our "inner man's" eyelids become droopy and we settle into a deep state of lethargy that leaves us sleepwalking through our days. We go through the motions, but our hearts and minds aren't in it. Breaking monotony's hold requires that we consciously direct our attention toward the Lord.

The Right Object

First, Moses focuses on the right object, the living God, the only One who can effectively break monotony's hold.

Lord, Thou hast been our dwelling place in all gener-
ations. (v. 1)

Like all Christians, Moses' prayer is a call home—it is a reaffir-
mation that God is our "dwelling place," our refuge. For us, to be
at home is to abide in Him.

The Right Perspective

The right focus then leads Moses to a right perspective that
safeguards against monotony's future encroachment.

Before the mountains were born,
Or Thou didst give birth to the earth and the world,
Even from everlasting to everlasting, Thou art God.
(v. 2)

Moses poetically broadens his perspective to see God's presence
in eternity past and future. It's His presence—at all times and places
—that gives our tasks, however menial, importance. It is not the
size of our tasks that gives them their significance, but the size of
our God.

Probing the Soul

Now Moses verbalizes three thoughts that often haunt us when
we feel like our lives are being spent on a monotonous treadmill.

My Life Is So Short

In verses 3–6 Moses holds up a collage of pictures depicting the
brevity of life.

Thou dost turn man back into dust,
And dost say, "Return, O children of men."
For a thousand years in Thy sight
Are like yesterday when it passes by,
Or as a watch in the night.
Thou hast swept them away like a flood, they fall asleep;
In the morning they are like grass which sprouts anew.
In the morning it flourishes, and sprouts anew;
Toward evening it fades, and withers away.

The specter of a short life spent attending monotonous details
haunts all of us who want our lives to amount to more than just a
period in the annals of time.

My Sins Are So Obvious

Next, Moses' attention is arrested by the conspicuousness of his sin.

For we have been consumed by Thine anger,
And by Thy wrath we have been dismayed.
Thou hast placed our iniquities before Thee,
Our secret sins in the light of Thy presence.
For all our days have declined in Thy fury;
We have finished our years like a sigh. (vv. 7–9)

During monotony's stagnating routines, our sins often seem to gather in plain view on the surface of our lives.

My Days Are Empty

Shadowing Moses' request in verse 12 is a sense of emptiness, prompted perhaps by the monotony in his life.

So teach us to number our days,
That we may present to Thee a heart of wisdom. (v. 12)

Like Moses, we are anxious to leave behind monotony's credo of insignificance to embrace the meaning that results in seeing life as God sees it.

Bringing the Song

As Moses ends his psalm, he asks for the Lord's presence and blessing.

Do return, O Lord; how long will it be?
And be sorry for Thy servants.
O satisfy us in the morning with Thy lovingkindness,
That we may sing for joy and be glad all our days.
Make us glad according to the days Thou hast afflicted us,
And the years we have seen evil.
Let Thy work appear to Thy servants,
And Thy majesty to their children.
And let the favor of the Lord our God be upon us;
And do confirm for us the work of our hands;
Yes, confirm the work of our hands. (vv. 13–17)

Moses asks God the question that persists on every family vacation: "How much longer?" Only this time Moses is putting into words the longing of all God's children who are under monotony's drone—we are anxious to know the *satisfaction* that comes from experiencing the Lord's understanding and support (vv. 13–14).

From there, Moses moves into the idea of *restoration*. We can certainly understand his request that Israel's present and future happiness come in direct proportion to past monotony and affliction (v. 15)! Moses then prays for the Lord to bring back their *motivation*, which, like ours, has a tendency to get bogged down by monotony (v. 16). Last, Moses asks for the *confirmation* we need as well—for God to help in seeing the significance of even their smallest tasks in light of His glorious plan (v. 17).

A Final Thought

Deep down inside all of us burns a desire whose heat can be felt in Thoreau's impassioned words,

I wanted to live deep and suck out all the marrow of life.[3]

But instead, monotony threatens to suck out all the marrow of *our* lives, to leave us with nothing but the dry, brittle bones of meaninglessness. So remember the things we have learned from Moses. And as Paul prayed,

Be strengthened with power through His Spirit in the inner man; so that Christ may dwell in your hearts through faith; and that you, being rooted and grounded in love, may be able to comprehend with all the saints what is the breadth and length and height and depth, and to know the love of Christ which surpasses knowledge, that you may be filled up to all the fulness of God. (Eph. 3:16b–19)

Living Insights

Did you know that Moses was a songwriter? As you've seen in this prayer-song, Psalm 90, the relationship of Moses with his God rings clear.

- This psalm is a picture in contrast. As an artist, Moses paints masterful strokes portraying God's power and man's frailty. Read through the seventeen verses slowly and look for references to both. Then record your observations in the space provided. When you conclude, try to write a one-sentence summary at the bottom of each section.

References to God's Power

_____

_____

3. Henry David Thoreau, *Thoreau: Walden and Other Writings*, p. 172.

_____

_____

_____

Summary: _____

_____

References to Man's Frailty

_____

_____

_____

_____

_____

Summary: _____

_____

 Living Insights   STUDY TWO

Any mom with summer vacationers knows the great wail of the ages: "Mom, there's nothing to do!" Boredom, sameness, weary routine . . . monotony lulls us to sleep. Well, splash some water in your face, because we're going to launch an all-out attack on dullness! Let's answer the following questions in order to learn how to best fight off monotony.

- What circumstances most often surround your life when you feel bored?

  1. _____

  _____

  2. _____

  _____

  3. _____

  _____

4. _____

_____

5. _____

_____

- Is it possible to change your circumstances in order to provide greater meaning during these times? If so, how?

  1. _____

  _____

  2. _____

  _____

  3. _____

  _____

  4. _____

  _____

  5. _____

  _____

Chapter 8

GROWING THROUGH FEAR
Psalm 27

Do you remember those dreaded oral book reports you had to give in school? Most of us probably don't recall what they were about or what we said. But we haven't forgotten the fear that roared in our hearts at those times. Names, faces, places—these have all faded from our minds. But not that fear.

Fortunately, we outgrow childish fears like monsters under our beds and ghosts in our closets. But we do not outgrow fear itself. The same fear that haunted us as children lives on inside of us as adults. The monsters and goblins have simply changed shapes to become visible to the adult eye. The specters that loom in front of us now come in the form of potential financial disasters, rebellious children, losing our marriage partners. The fear is just as real, just as scary.

Fear makes our world smaller. When it attacks in a particular area of our lives, we tend to pull back, retreat, rather than meet it head-on. We hide at home, sleep, overeat, make excuses . . . anything to avoid the problem. We just don't want to face it. And so the boundaries of our world shrink a little more. As Paul Tournier suggests in his book *The Strong and the Weak,* all of us have reservoirs of full potential—vast areas of great satisfaction. But the roads that lead to those reservoirs "are guarded by the dragon of fear."[1]

If you find yourself cowering before the dragon of fear, David knows how you feel. He's been crippled by it too. Yes, he was the king of Israel, the one who slew Goliath. And yes, he was chosen by God to be king, and he led Israel to great heights in prosperity. But while he was accomplishing all that, he also had to overcome many of the same fears that camp on our doorsteps.

In Psalm 27, David gives us an inside look at how he dealt with fear.

---

1. Paul Tournier, *The Strong and the Weak,* trans. Edwin Hudson (Philadelphia, Pa.: Westminster Press, n.d.), p. 93.

An Overall Glance

In most of the Psalms a superscription, or explanatory note, is given after the title. In our modern translations of the Bible, the superscription under Psalm 27 says "A Psalm of David." But in the earliest Greek version, called the Septuagint, the superscription takes the explanation a little farther: "A Psalm of David Before He Was Anointed." David was anointed twice in his lifetime—once as a teenager by the prophet Samuel, signifying he was to be Israel's future king, and a second time when he actually became king and sat on the throne. Even though the superscription doesn't specifically say, the text seems to indicate that Psalm 27 was written before his second anointing, when he was the object of Saul's hatred and spear.

Scope of the Psalm

Psalm 27 can easily be divided into two contrasting sections. In verses 1–6 David exudes a confidence that comes from keeping his faith trained on God. In verses 7–14 the mood shifts, and we begin to hear from a David whose faith has been replaced with fear.

Outline of the Psalm

Let's take a moment to glance at a map of the psalm's geography and discover the main trails that David's thoughts blaze.

The first verse gives us the *theme*, which reverberates throughout the psalm: Because the Lord is my light, salvation, and defense, I have no fear. In the following four verses, David makes a *declaration of trust* (vv. 2–6). At the next juncture, David detours from the path of faith to the path of fear. In these verses, 7–14, we find a *prayer for strength* as David admits his dependence and weakness. In verse 14 David finally finds his footing, as he concludes with a *reminder to wait on the Lord.*

An Internal Analysis

Now we are ready to make a close inspection of David's words, without "losing the psalm for the verses"!

Theme

David leads us into the psalm's theme by using two similar statements, each followed by questions with obvious answers.

> The Lord is my light and my salvation;
> Whom shall I fear?
> The Lord is the defense of my life;
> Whom shall I dread? (Ps. 27:1)

INSIGHT FOR LIVING

Broadcast Schedule

October 12–November 2, 1989

Growing Pains

Thursday	October 12	**Growing through Waiting** Psalm 62:1–2, 5–8
Friday	October 13	**Growing through Waiting**
Monday	October 16	**Growing through Failure** Psalm 103
Tuesday	October 17	**Growing through Failure**
Wednesday	October 18	**Growing through Misunderstanding** Psalm 140
Thursday	October 19	**Growing through Misunderstanding**
Friday	October 20	**Growing through Loss** Job 1–2
Monday	October 23	**Growing through Loss**
Tuesday	October 24	**Growing through Mistakes** Psalm 31, Selected Scripture
Wednesday	October 25	**Growing through Mistakes**
Thursday	October 26	**Growing through Weakness** Psalm 46
Friday	October 27	**Growing through Weakness**
Monday	October 30	**Growing through Monotony** Psalm 90
Tuesday	October 31	**Growing through Monotony**
Wednesday	November 1	**Growing through Fear** Psalm 27
Thursday	November 2	**Growing through Fear**

The first question uses the common, everyday Hebrew word for *fear;* it simply indicates "anxiety or agitation." But in the second question, the word used for *dread* is *pachad,* which is a less common Hebrew word that means "to be in awe, intimidated, or filled with dread."

Declaration of Trust

Next, David flips through a scrapbook of intimidating situations that he has had to face in real life.

> When evildoers came upon me to devour my flesh,
> My adversaries and my enemies, they stumbled and
>   fell.
> Though a host encamp against me,
> My heart will not fear;
> Though war arise against me,
> In spite of this I shall be confident. (vv. 2–3)

Talk about intimidation! Saul's entire army was out to get one man—David. And he had no place to hide. Even his mother and father had turned their backs on him.

> For my father and my mother have forsaken me.
> (v. 10a)

The circumstances in David's life were numerous enough and strong enough to break down the doors to his heart and force him to become a slave of fear. But David's defenses held fast, because he was "confident" (v. 3). The Hebrew word used for *confident* here is *batach.* It doesn't mean "self-confident" or "clever." It means, instead, "to be secure, to have assurance." In spite of all the rejection and intimidation, David was able to feel secure because he put his trust in the Lord.

> One thing I have asked from the Lord, that I shall seek:
> That I may dwell in the house of the Lord all the days
>   of my life,
> To behold the beauty of the Lord,
> And to meditate in His temple.
> For in the day of trouble He will conceal me in His
>   tabernacle;
> In the secret place of His tent He will hide me;
> He will lift me up on a rock.
> And now my head will be lifted up above my enemies
>   around me;
> And I will offer in His tent sacrifices with shouts of joy;
> I will sing, yes, I will sing praises to the Lord. (vv. 4–6)

In these three verses, David portrays fellowship with God as being like living in God's dwelling place. Though he could not be there literally, David knew that his heart and mind could shelter themselves behind the walls of God's strength and assurance.

Prayer for Support

In a rather abrupt change, David's words switch from an expression of what he desires to the expression of his gut-level feelings—fear and desperation.

> Hear, O Lord, when I cry with my voice,
> And be gracious to me and answer me.
> When Thou didst say, "Seek My face," my heart said
> to Thee,
> "Thy face, O Lord, I shall seek."
> Do not hide Thy face from me,
> Do not turn Thy servant away in anger;
> Thou hast been my help;
> Do not abandon me nor forsake me,
> O God of my salvation! (vv. 7–9)

This is no half-hearted petition! David isn't thinking about other options he might pursue as he prays. His words possess a boldness and fervency of one not afraid of trusting absolutely in God (see also Phil. 4:6–7 and Heb. 4:16).

> Teach me Thy way, O Lord,
> And lead me in a level path,
> Because of my foes.
> Do not deliver me over to the desire of my adversaries;
> For false witnesses have risen against me,
> And such as breathe out violence.
> I would have despaired unless I had believed that I
> would see the goodness of the Lord
> In the land of the living. (Ps. 27:11–13)

Encouragement to Wait

The last verse of David's psalm brings us back full circle to where we began our study of growing pains—to waiting. David recognizes that there's nothing he can do to solve his problem with Saul. He can only turn to the Lord, where he will find the confidence he needs to face his fears.

A Practical Response

As we step out of David's world back into our own, let's not forget to bring with us some of the practical advice he has to offer concerning our fears.

First: *As fears occur, admit them.* Get in the habit of expressing your specific fears to the Lord. Don't be afraid to acknowledge them!

Second: *As you admit them, commit them.* To the best of your ability, hand your fears to the Lord, as David did, without reservation, without double-checking other options. Just let them go.

Third: *As you commit them, release them.* Don't allow fear to settle down and get comfortable in any room of your heart.

Fourth: *As you release them, resist them.* Those same fears you gave to the Lord yesterday can come knocking on your door today. Keep a careful and constant watch on all the doors to your heart.

Fifth: *As you resist them, stand firm.* Don't let those fears chase you away from the solid ground of God's protection.

A Final Thought

What many little children love about the game of hide-and-seek is not the hiding, it's the being found. Oftentimes they will even tell you where they are so that you'll be sure to find them!

In a way, we are all like that. We live in the darkness of a sinful world, and we get plain scared at times. Fears overwhelm us, and we have that same yearning of a little child wanting to be found. We long to be assured that God knows exactly where we are and that He will come to lift us into His arms and calm our fears like He calmed the waters.

> "Can a woman forget her nursing child,
> And have no compassion on the son of her womb?
> Even these may forget, but I will not forget you.
> Behold, I have inscribed you on the palms of My hands."
> (Isa. 49:15–16a)

55

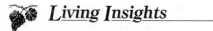

Living *Insights*

The dragon of fear breathes fire on us all. Everyone has a pet fear. It may be large or small, but either way it is significant in our lives.

- Let's zero in on that pet fear and seek to bring some relief to its hold on us.

  1. Start by admitting your fear. Identify it and openly call it by name.

  2. Next, commit that fear to the Lord. The Lord awaits this, so give it to Him.

  3. Think through very carefully what you can do to resist the fear's return, and write down a plan to bring future victory.

  _____

  _____

  _____

  _____

  4. Reread Psalm 27 and ask God for strength in this area of your life.

Living *Insights*

There's no gain without pain. Are you in the growing process? Does it sometimes hurt? I'm sure that, through these studies, you've gained a clearer focus on God's view of growth and seen His hand in these eight areas of discomfort. Let's look back and review some main points.

- Listed below are the eight topics covered in this series. Write down the strongest thought you can recall about each. Then, jot down how you'll approach each problem area differently as a result of this study. In this way, you can move from growing pains to maturity.

Waiting

Thoughts: _____

_____

Approach: _____

_____

Failure

Thoughts: _____

_____

Approach: _____

_____

Misunderstanding

Thoughts: _____

_____

Approach: _____

_____

Loss

Thoughts: _____

_____

Approach: _____

_____

Mistakes

Thoughts: _____

_____

Approach: _____

_____

Weakness

Thoughts: _____

_____

Approach: _____

_____

Monotony

Thoughts: _____

_____

Approach: _____

_____

Fear

Thoughts: _____

_____

Approach: _____

_____

BOOKS FOR
PROBING FURTHER

Most of us wouldn't mind learning about growing pains in a temperature-controlled classroom on a university campus. We could handle having a set curriculum with scheduled tests and the freedom to choose what subjects we would take, and when.

But in the school of growing pains, you don't always get the subject you want at the time you want it. In addition, that school has a reputation for holding classes in places you wouldn't pick at temperatures that are never comfortable. The tests are hard and given without warning, and the curriculum is unpredictable.

Though none of us like majoring in growing pains, the reality is that we will never mature without the pain of fear, misunderstandings, losses, failure, and the rest. We hope that these lessons have provided you with the hope, insight, and encouragement you need to continue pursuing Christ. For further assistance in learning how to deal with growing pains, we would recommend these books.

Augsburger, David. *The Freedom of Forgiveness.* Chicago, Ill.: Moody Press, 1988. The author combines personal testimonies with Scripture for a highly motivational guide for applying forgiveness in your life.

Barber, Cyril J., and Sharalee Aspenleiter. *Through the Valley of Tears.* Old Tappan, N.J.: Fleming H. Revell Co., 1987. For those of you grieving over the loss of a loved one, the authors walk through each stage of the grieving process with you. In doing so, they provide practical biblical advice and assurance of God's abiding love.

Crabb, Larry, and Dan B. Allender. *Encouragement: The Key to Caring.* Grand Rapids, Mich.: Zondervan Publishing House, Pyranee Books, 1984. We all need not only to receive encouragement, but also to know how to give it. The authors provide us with some seasoned insights into people's pain and the practical skills to begin encouraging others more effectively.

Crabb, Larry. *Inside Out.* Colorado Springs, Colo.: NavPress, 1988. Dr. Crabb challenges us to take off our picture-perfect masks of pretension and face the inner problems that sidetrack us from truly living for God.

Lutzer, Erwin W. *Failure: The Back Door to Success.* Chicago, Ill.: Moody Press, 1975. With sensitivity, understanding, and encouragement, Lutzer helps those who have been flattened by failure to find God's grace to get up.

Swindoll, Charles R. *Three Steps Forward, Two Steps Back.* Nashville, Tenn.: Thomas Nelson Publishers, 1980. Chuck looks at the side of our lives that is darkened by difficult problems and disappointments. In a down-to-earth way, he confronts reality and its hurts and then holds out hope for those who learn to persevere.

Wright, H. Norman. *Communication: Key to Your Marriage.* Glendale, Calif.: G/L Publications, Regal Books, 1974. Whether you're married or single, this book will be of tremendous practical value in improving your ability to communicate. It's a very relevant book written in a warm personal style.

Yancey, Philip. *Disappointment with God.* Grand Rapids, Mich.: Zondervan Publishing House, 1988. Yancey deals insightfully with the questions that nag all of us during our growing pains: Is God unfair? Is God silent? Is God hidden? You will find this a sensitive and encouraging book.

Insight for Living
Cassette Tapes
GROWING PAINS

Eight of the most difficult and frustrating tests in life are addressed in this series of practical talks. Realism and honesty characterize each one. If you are tired of clichés and weary of empty promises that ignore the dark side of life, *Growing Pains* is for you. You will discover there are ways to cope (and even grow!) through tough times of trouble.

			U.S.	Canada
GRP	CS	Cassette series—includes album cover ..	$23.75	$30.00
		Individual cassettes—include messages A and B	5.00	6.35

These prices are subject to change without notice.

GRP 1-A: *Growing through Waiting*—Psalm 62:1–2, 5–8
   B: *Growing through Failure*—Psalm 103

GRP 2-A: *Growing through Misunderstanding*—Psalm 140
   B: *Growing through Loss*—Job 1–2

GRP 3-A: *Growing through Mistakes*—Psalm 31, Selected Scripture
   B: *Growing through Weakness*—Psalm 46

GRP 4-A: *Growing through Monotony*—Psalm 90
   B: *Growing through Fear*—Psalm 27

How to Order by Mail

Simply mark on the order form whether you want the series or individual tapes. Mail the form with your payment to the appropriate address listed below. We will process your order as promptly as we can.

United States: Mail your order to the Sales Department at Insight for Living, Post Office Box 4444, Fullerton, California 92634. If you wish your order to be shipped first-class for faster delivery, add 10 percent of the total order amount (not including California sales tax). Otherwise, please allow four to six weeks for delivery by fourth-class mail. We accept personal checks, money orders, Visa, or MasterCard in payment for materials. Unfortunately, we are unable to offer invoicing or COD orders.

Canada: Mail your order to Insight for Living Ministries, Post Office Box 2510, Vancouver, British Columbia V6B 3W7. Please add 7 percent of your total order for first-class postage and allow approximately four weeks for delivery. Our listeners in British Columbia must also add a 6 percent sales tax to the total of all tape orders (not including postage). We accept personal checks, money orders, Visa, or MasterCard in payment for materials. Unfortunately, we are unable to offer invoicing or COD orders.

Australia, New Zealand, or Papua New Guinea: Mail your order to Insight for Living, Inc., GPO Box 2823 EE, Melbourne, Victoria 3001, Australia. Please allow six to ten weeks for delivery by surface mail. If you would like your order sent airmail, the delivery time may be reduced. Whether you choose surface or airmail, postage costs must be added to the amount of purchase and included with your order. Please use the chart that follows to determine correct postage. Due to fluctuating currency rates, we can accept only personal checks made payable in U.S. funds, international money orders, Visa, or MasterCard in payment for materials.

Overseas: Other overseas residents should contact our U.S. office. Please allow six to ten weeks for delivery by surface mail. If you would like your order sent airmail, the delivery time may be reduced. Whether you choose surface or airmail, postage costs must be added to the amount of purchase and included with your order. Please use the chart that follows to determine correct postage. Due to fluctuating currency rates, we can accept only personal checks made payable in U.S. funds, international money orders, Visa, or MasterCard in payment for materials.

Type of Postage	Postage Cost
Surface	10% of total order
Airmail	25% of total order

For Faster Service, Order by Telephone

To purchase using Visa or MasterCard, you are welcome to use our **toll-free** numbers between the hours of 8:30 A.M. and 4:00 P.M., Pacific time, Monday through Friday. The number to call from anywhere in the United States is **1-800-772-8888.** To order from Canada, call our Vancouver office at **1-800-663-7639.** Vancouver residents should call (604) 272-5811. Telephone orders from overseas are handled through our Sales Department at (714) 870-9161. We are unable to accept collect calls.

Our Guarantee

Our cassettes are guaranteed for ninety days against faulty performance or breakage due to a defect in the tape. For best results, please be sure your tape recorder is in good operating condition and is cleaned regularly.

Note: To cover processing and handling, there is a $10 fee for *any* returned check.

Order Form

GRP CS represents the entire *Growing Pains* series, while GRP 1–4 are the individual tapes included in the series.

Series or Tape	Unit Price U.S.	Unit Price Canada	Quantity	Amount
GRP CS	$23.75	$30.00		$
GRP 1	5.00	6.35		
GRP 2	5.00	6.35		
GRP 3	5.00	6.35		
GRP 4	5.00	6.35		
			Subtotal	
			Sales tax *6% for orders delivered in California or British Columbia*	
			Postage *7% in Canada; overseas residents, see "How to Order by Mail"*	
			10% optional first-class shipping and handling *U.S. residents only*	
			Gift to Insight for Living *Tax-deductible in the U.S. and Canada*	
			Total amount due *Please do not send cash.*	$

If there is a balance: ☐ apply it as a donation ☐ please refund

Form of payment:

☐ Check or money order made payable to Insight for Living

☐ Credit card (circle one):   Visa   MasterCard

Card Number _____ Expiration Date _____

Signature _____
We cannot process your credit card purchase without your signature.

Name _____

Address _____

City _____

State/Province_____ Zip/Postal Code _____

Country _____

Telephone _(____)_____ Radio Station ____ ____ ____ ____
If questions arise concerning your order, we may need to contact you.

Mail this order form to the Sales Department at one of these addresses:
Insight for Living, Post Office Box 4444, Fullerton, CA 92634
Insight for Living Ministries, Post Office Box 2510, Vancouver, BC, Canada V6B 3W7
Insight for Living, Inc., GPO Box 2823 EE, Melbourne, VIC 3001, Australia

Order Form

GRP CS represents the entire *Growing Pains* series, while GRP 1–4 are the individual tapes included in the series.

Series or Tape	Unit Price U.S.	Unit Price Canada	Quantity	Amount
GRP CS	$23.75	$30.00		$
GRP 1	5.00	6.35		
GRP 2	5.00	6.35		
GRP 3	5.00	6.35		
GRP 4	5.00	6.35		
			Subtotal	
			Sales tax *6% for orders delivered in California or British Columbia*	
			Postage *7% in Canada; overseas residents, see "How to Order by Mail"*	
			10% optional first-class shipping and handling *U.S. residents only*	
			Gift to Insight for Living *Tax-deductible in the U.S. and Canada*	
			Total amount due *Please do not send cash.*	$

If there is a balance: ☐ apply it as a donation ☐ please refund

Form of payment:

☐ Check or money order made payable to Insight for Living

☐ Credit card (circle one): Visa MasterCard

Card Number _____ Expiration Date _____

Signature _____
We cannot process your credit card purchase without your signature.

Name _____

Address _____

City _____

State/Province_____ Zip/Postal Code _____

Country _____

Telephone ( ) _____ Radio Station ___ ___ ___ ___
If questions arise concerning your order, we may need to contact you.

Mail this order form to the Sales Department at one of these addresses:
Insight for Living, Post Office Box 4444, Fullerton, CA 92634
Insight for Living Ministries, Post Office Box 2510, Vancouver, BC, Canada V6B 3W7
Insight for Living, Inc., GPO Box 2823 EE, Melbourne, VIC 3001, Australia